Copyright © 2024, Diana Plavnieva. All rights reserved.
English Language editor © Anastasiia Kondratieva

No part of this book may be reproduced, distributed, or transmitted in any form without permission from the publisher, except as permitted by U.S. copyright law.

For permission contact: dianaplavneva@gmail.com

Table of Contents

Introduction 4
Inspiring Stories 5
Part 1: Creating a Vision Board 6
   1.1. Preparation Stage: 4 Key Elements 6
   1.2. The Creation Process: Step by Step 9
Part 2: Categories of Life and the Art of Desiring 10
   2.1. Defining the Basic Categories of Life according to Bagua 10
   2.2. How to Write down your Dreams 12
Part 3: Compiling a List of 100 Desires 13
   3.1 Health: The Key to Energy and Strength 13
   3.2. Relationships: The Element of Harmony 25
   3.3. Creativity & Children: Sources of Inspiration and Joy 35
   3.4. Helpful people & Travel: Allies in Exploring the World 45
   3.5. Career: The Path to Success and Self-Realization 57
   3.6. Knowledge: Development and Learning 65
   3.7. Family: Strengthening Bonds with Loved Ones 71
   3.8. Wealth: The Path to Financial Freedom 79
   3.9. Fame: Recognition and Influence 91
Part 4: Enhancing Effectiveness 101
   4.1. The Practice of Gratitude: The Key to Success 101
   4.2. The Technique of Powerful Visualization: The Path to Realizing a Dream 101
Conclusion 103

Introduction

Many people believe that they need resources like money, people, and time to achieve their goals. However, **the most important resource is within us.**

Our brain is wired to follow the principle of **"See first — believe later."** This determines our perception and influences our behavior. We tend to believe in things that we can see, even if they are trivial or harmful.

We often fear negative outcomes and imagine worst-case scenarios. However, it is not our fault. This is how our brain is designed. We need to see something to be able to believe in it.

But are we able to see electricity, radiation or 3 million bacteria on our skin? We can only see these things through devices. So, when it comes to real life, the principle is exactly the opposite: **"Believe first — see later."**

To achieve our desires, our brain needs to work in this manner. We must rewire our brain to change our beliefs. **This is where visualization comes in.**

Everything in this world, from the ballpoint pen to the house you live in, was once just an idea that somebody believed in. The idea was put into words, and only after that, it materialized in the physical world.

The second important aspect of visualization is positive emotions. These emotions serve as our engine, our energy. We need them to boost our personal power and achieve our goals.

In conclusion, the power of visualization lies in **turning our desires into intentions**, using our internal resources, and shifting our brain's default program from **"See first — believe later"** to the innovative and powerful **"Believe first — see later."**

Inspiring Stories

Story 1:

It's hard to believe what a native of the small Austrian town of Thal has achieved without even knowing English... From a young age, Arnold Schwarzenegger envisioned what he wanted to be: "When I was young, I visualized myself being and having what it was I wanted. Mentally I never had any doubts about it. The mind is really so incredible. Before I won my first Mr. Universe, I walked around the tournament like I owned it. The title was already mine. I had won it so many times in my mind that there was no doubt I would win it. Then when I moved on to the movies, the same thing. I visualize myself being a successful actor and earning big money. I could feel and taste success. I just knew it would all happen."

Story 2:

My friend Kelly dreamed of selling her business to have more free time. She visualized spending more time with her family and children. A few days later, fate gave her a gift in the most unexpected situation when an encounter on her way to the restroom changed her life. The stranger was looking for a completely different business, but Kelly saw it as a sign and decided to offer hers. This decision became a turning point in her life: the man she met by chance was a perfect buyer, and the deal was made within a week.

Story 3:

One of my personal vivid stories of visualization is how I joined a travelers' club and added the dream of visiting the Maldives to my favorites. I would often fall asleep and see myself walking on these paradise islands, talking about them so much that even my boyfriend got inspired by the idea and set the wallpaper on his phone. After a year and a half, we visited the Maldives despite the global COVID-19 pandemic.

These inspiring stories prove the undeniable power of visualization in achieving goals. They remind us that our thoughts and dreams can become a reality if we channel them in the right direction.

Now that you know about this powerful tool that can change your life, it's time to act!

Part 1: Creating a Vision Board

1.1. Preparation Stage: 4 Key Elements

#1 Time

Allocate enough time — more than 4 hours. The ideal time for this is during the waxing moon phase. Lunar cycles are believed to affect the energy of the Earth and people. This is the perfect time for new beginnings and attracting new opportunities.

#2 Place

Organize a space where you will not be distracted. You need a place that fosters concentration and calmness.

#3 Materials

Prepare additional materials: scissors, glue, and a board base (e.g., a piece of cardboard, a large sheet of paper, a wooden board).

#4 Emotional State

Enter into one of these resourceful states, or fill yourself with all of them:
Anticipation: imagine how your life will change.
Unreasonable Joy: think about how "it's just nice to be alive."
Delight: feel the beauty of the world.
Determination: act without doubt; the decision has already been made.
Celebration of Victory: imagine how you have achieved success.
Kindness: be kind to yourself, the world, and the people around you.

2025 MOON CALENDAR

January
6 13 21 29

February
5 12 20 27

March
6 14 22 29

April
5 12 20 27

May
4 12 20 26

June
2 11 18 25

July
2 10 17 24

August
1 9 16 23 31

September
7 14 21 29

October
6 13 21 29

November
5 12 20 28

December
4 11 19 27

New Moon   First Quarter   Full Moon   Third Quarter

1.2. The Creation Process: Step by Step

Creating a vision board is a powerful way to visualize your goals and dreams, turning them from abstract ideas into concrete images and words that motivate you daily to move forward. Here is a step-by-step guide to creating a vision board:

Step 1: Define Your Goals

The first step is to clearly define your goals and desires. Think about what you want to achieve in different aspects of your life and write them down on the wish forms provided in this book.

Step 2: Cut Out Relevant Elements

Cut out images and words from magazines that accurately reflect your goals and desires.

Step 3: Arrange the Elements

Before gluing anything, arrange the elements on the board to see how they fit together. This will help you balance the space and create a harmonious visual sequence.

Step 4: Attach the Elements

Once you are satisfied with the arrangement, start gluing the elements onto the board. You can also add handwritten notes, quotes, or any other words that inspire you.

Step 5: Place the Board

Place your vision board where you will see it every day. It could be in your bedroom, home office, or anywhere else within your sight.

Step 6: Update the Board

As you reach your goals or your desires change, update the board. It is a dynamic tool that should grow and change along with you.

Step 7: Express Gratitude

Thank the Universe for every wish that comes true.

Step 8: Visualize Your Goals

The vision board is not just a decoration. It is a tool for achieving goals. Regularly look at it, imagine achieving your goals, and let these images inspire you.

Part 2: Categories of Life and the Art of Desiring

2.1. Defining the Basic Categories of Life according to Bagua

The most effective technique for creating a vision board is using the Bagua diagram from the ancient Chinese Feng Shui science. The Bagua diagram helps harmonize life through a balanced distribution of resources across all aspects of life. Each aspect corresponds to its own cardinal direction and color.

According to ancient teaching, the Bagua diagram was octagonal, as temples in Asia were built in a similar shape. Over time, people adapted the Bagua diagram by adding another sector and changing its size to match the shape of living spaces. Thus, the rectangle became part of our everyday lives.

The primary purpose of the Bagua diagram is to activate sectors so that harmony and happiness enter a person's life. If objects in space are arranged correctly, the Qi energy (life force, part of the universal energy) will flow freely and bring what is desired into life.

Using the Bagua diagram helps you divide your life into vital values and understand what you truly want in each area **in equal proportion without focusing solely on material goods.**

Currently, the standard Bagua diagram consists of 9 sectors:
- Health
- Relationships
- Creativity & Children
- Helpful People & Travel
- Career
- Knowledge
- Family
- Wealth
- Fame.

Bagua diagram

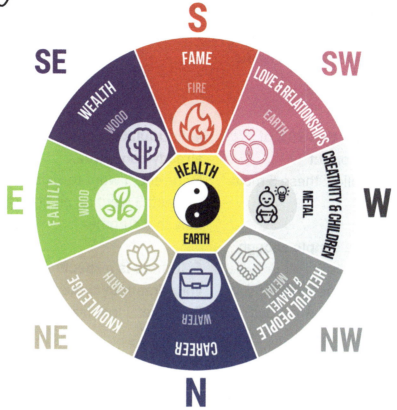

How to make Vision Board using Bagua diagram

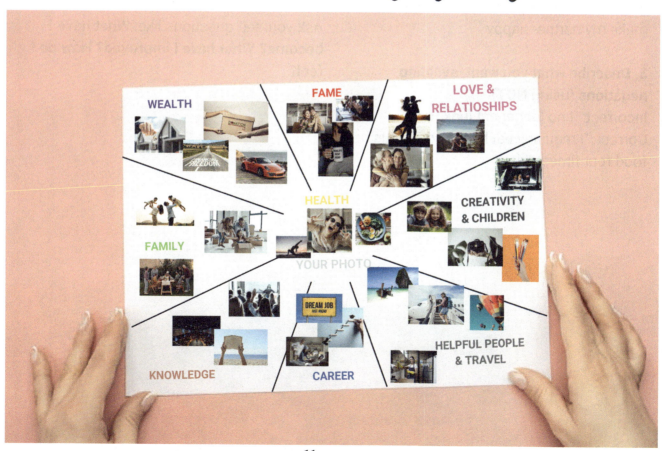

2.2. How to Write down your Dreams

It is important to remember that 99% of success depends on the correct formulation of desires. Follow these 5 main rules:

1. The first wish should be simple enough to be realized in the first week.
This will create a positive experience and motivation for achieving more ambitious goals.
Example: "I had a great time with my family. We went to the cinema for the premiere of a new movie."

2. Your wish is about yourself.
Incorrect: "My partner makes me happy."
Correct: "I am happy in my marriage and make my partner happy."

3. Describe what you want, avoiding negations (using NOT).
Incorrect: "I no longer eat junk food."
Correct: "I regularly eat healthy delicious food four times a day."

4. Formulate wishes as if they have already come true.
Incorrect: "I want to visit Italy."
Correct: "I went on an unforgettable trip to Italy this summer."

5. If there is a specific time when you want your dream to come true, write about it.
Example: "I lost 5 kg over the next 3 months."

If you find it difficult to recall your desires, look at the pictures. They will help you formulate what you dream about. You can also cut them out right away.

Ask yourself questions like: **What have I become? What have I improved? How do I feel?**

Part 3: Compiling a List of 100 Desires

3.1. Health: The Key to Energy and Strength

Write down 10 wishes below related to improving your physical condition, such as regular workouts and healthy eating. Also, write down goals related to strengthening your mental health, such as meditation and therapy sessions. Also include wishes about beauty (body, teeth, hair, etc).

Here are some examples to help you get started:

- I always maintain a resourceful state by enjoying myself in all areas of life.
- I've improved my physical body by working out in the gym three times a week.
- I've started practicing yoga twice a week.
- I've improved my sleep by going to bed at 10:00 PM, ensuring I get at least 8 hours of sleep every night.
- I enjoy eating delicious and healthy food, and plan my weekly menu.
- I've lost 10 kg thanks to proper nutrition and increased physical activity.
- I drink more than 2 liters of water every day.
- I practise meditation for 10 minutes every morning.
- I have beautiful well-groomed hair thanks to keratin straightening.
- I go for a massage once a week.

Health Wish List

○ 1

○ 2

○ 3

○ 4

○ 5

○ 6

○ 7

○ 8

○ 9

○ 10

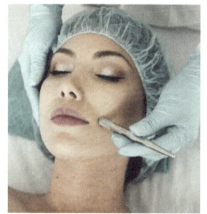

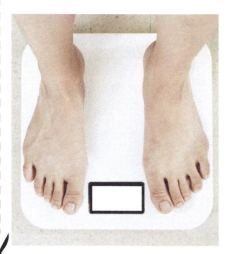

Wellness

Balance

Harmony

Recovery

Mindfulness

grateful thankful blessed

keep balance

ENERGY

GRL PWR

POWERFUL

Enjoy life

EMBRAVE. EMBRACE. EMPOWER.

Happiness is the choice

it's TIME TO Relax

SHINE BRIGHT LIKE a DIAMOND

I attract positive energy

keep going

YOU can DO IT

NEVER GIVE UP

ALL BODIES are GOOD BODIES

I choose joy and positivity

I DO IT FOR ME

WAKE UP AND workout

My body is healthy and vibrant

MY POTENTIAL IS ENDLESS

I radiate confidence and calm

I AM WORTHY OF MY DREAMS

Fearless

Grateful

enjoy every moment.

Live WITHOUT REGRETS

I RELEASE ALL DOUBTS AND FEARS

"Rule your mind or it will rule you."

It always SEEMS IMPOSSIBLE until IT'S DONE

→ believe →

I CAN CHANGE THE WORLD

YES!

I AM A MAGNET FOR MIRACLES

3.2. Relationships: The Element of Harmony

Write down 10 wishes below related to improving relationships with your partner, friends, family, and colleagues.

Examples:

- I'm happy in my relationship and make my partner happy by regularly paying attention to the needs and desires and making sure we create happy memories together.
- I've taken a romantic trip with my partner.
- I've improved my ability to express my feelings and emotions, which strengthened my romantic relationship.
- I've improved my relationship with my parents; now we spend more free time together.
- I've made new friends by participating in communities and events with like-minded people.
- I've reconciled with an old friend by taking the initiative to resolve past disagreements and demonstrating a willingness to compromise, which allowed us to renew our friendship.
- I got used to living in a new city by actively meeting new people and participating in local events, which allowed me to build a new circle of friends and feel part of the community.
- I've established healthy relationships with colleagues by working on joint projects and maintaining a positive work atmosphere.
- I've achieved work-life balance, which positively affected my relationships.
- I've learned to forgive, which helped me let go of grudges and improve my relationships.

Relationships Wish List

○ 1

○ 2

○ 3

○ 4

○ 5

○ 6

○ 7

○ 8

○ 9

○ 10

TRUST

PASSION

JOY

Love

Happiness

ALL YOU NEED IS *Love*

love GROWS *here*

"Where there is love there is life."

best friends

I AM A MAGNET FOR POSITIVE RELATIONSHIPS

True friends are like diamonds – bright, beautiful, valuable, and always in style.

MY HEART IS OPEN TO LOVE

I am worthy of love

LOVE IS IN THE *air*

Love surrounds me and everyone around me

"Life is the flower for which love is the honey."

MY RELATIONSHIPS ARE GROUNDED IN TRUST AND RESPECT

I'M LOVED FOR WHO I AM

choose love

I AM GRATEFUL FOR THE LOVE IN MY LIFE

KEEP *calm* AND *love*

I offer and receive love freely

love TO THE moon AND BACK

MY RELATIONSHIPS ARE FULL OF HARMONY AND JOY

YOU *Make* TODAY BETTER

3.3. Creativity & Children: Sources of Inspiration and Joy

Write down 10 wishes below related to developing creative skills, such as engaging in art, music, writing, or other creative pursuits. Include new hobbies that bring joy and broaden horizons. If you have children or spend a lot of time with them, feel free to include wishes related to them as well.

Examples:

- I've learned to play the guitar.
- I've taken up dancing.
- I've learned to paint with watercolors.
- I've learned to edit videos for my blog.
- I've mastered culinary arts and now treat my loved ones to new dishes every week.
- I've taken up rock climbing and completed several climbs of intermediate difficulty.
- I've successfully developed my YouTube channel about DIY projects, reaching over 10,000 subscribers by collaborating with famous brands.
- I've managed to instill a love for reading in my children by regularly reading to them before bedtime.
- I've successfully taught my children financial literacy basics, which helps them confidently manage their pocket money.
- I've organized a trip for my children that broadened their outlook.

Creativity & Children Wish List

1.
2.
3.
4.
5.
6.
7.
8.
9.
10.

 **K** Followers

@
K Following

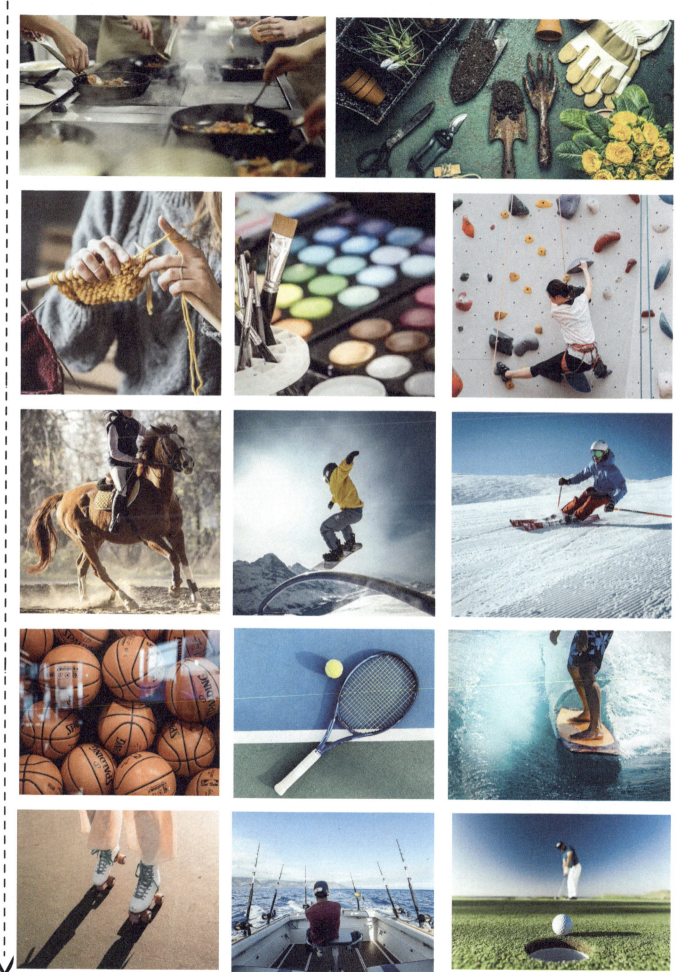

IMAGINE

DREAM

CREATE

Innovation

Inspiration

DON'T THINK
OUTSIDE THE BOX.
THINK LIKE
THERE IS NO BOX.

Be **Creative**

I can do Anything

MY IMAGINATION IS BOUNDLESS

Creativity flows through me

" THE PAINTER HAS THE UNIVERSE IN HIS MIND AND HANDS "

Dream Big

" Art, freedom and creativity will change society faster than politics "

NEW IDEAS COME TO ME EASILY

Don't Stop!

I'm inspired by the world around me

I'm open to creative inspiration

3.4. Helpful people & Travel: Allies in Exploring the World

Write down 10 wishes below related to the help and support you need to achieve your goals. Mentors, coaches, and therapists can be valuable allies in both your personal and professional lives. Integrating new technology and delegating tasks to others can significantly simplify and automate your daily routine. Additionally, include your travel wishes, as they are a form of support for implementing your plans.

Examples:

- I have a mentor with experience in my professional field and we meet on a weekly basis.
- I regularly take Spanish lessons with a tutor.
- I've found a stylist who helped me create a new wardrobe.
- I've found a healthy lifestyle mentor whose advice helped me improve my physical condition and overall well-being.
- I have a personal fitness trainer.
- I've hired a nanny to pick up my children from school and stay with them for a few hours.
- I've found a convenient program for organizing my tasks.
- I've hired a qualified assistant to delegate routine tasks, allowing me to concentrate on more important strategic goals.
- I've brought a new manager to the team, which freed up more of my time and improved my performance.
- I enjoy exploring new places and embracing new experiences while traveling.

Helpful People & Travel Wish List

◯ 1 _____
_____

◯ 2 _____
_____

◯ 3 _____
_____

◯ 4 _____
_____

◯ 5 _____
_____

◯ 6 _____
_____

◯ 7 _____
_____

◯ 8 _____
_____

◯ 9 _____
_____

◯ 10 _____
_____

France

Japan

Australia

Italy

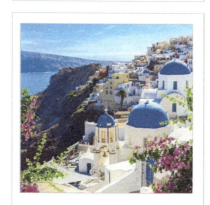
Greece

Great Britain

Spain

Emirates

Thailand

Holland

Norway

Iceland

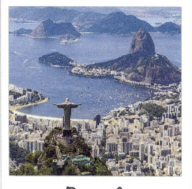
Brazil

Maldives

South Africa

Indonesia

Egypt

Canada

New York

San Francisco

Las Vegas

Arizona

Los Angeles

Hawaii

Mentor

Support

Adventure

Discover

Explore

I'M GRATEFUL FOR THE SUPPORT I RECEIVE DAILY

I'm blessed with mentors who guide me

I DESERVE AND RECEIVE HELP WHENEVER I NEED IT

Every trip enriches my life

I explore new places with an open heart

3.5. Career: The Path to Success and Self-Realization

Write down 10 wishes below related to increasing your income, advancing your career, expanding a business, starting your own business, developing a startup, or participating in investment projects.

Examples:

- My annual income is more than $100,000.
- I've received an offer for an extra monthly income of more than $500.
- I've optimized my work hours to 5 hours a day.
- I've been promoted to a managerial position.
- I've initiated and successfully implemented an innovative project within the company.
- I've created and developed my online craft store, bringing in a steady income.
- I've launched my culinary online course.
- I've expanded my business by opening a second office in a new city, which led to a 50% increase in income and the client base expansion.
- I've formed a team of qualified specialists.
- I've organized a summer corporate event for the team, where we joyfully celebrated our achievements.

Career Wish List

○ 1

○ 2

○ 3

○ 4

○ 5

○ 6

○ 7

○ 8

○ 9

○ 10

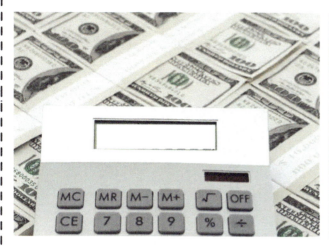

SUCCESS

LEADERSHIP

INCOME

Strategy

Productivity

MY WORK BRINGS ME JOY AND FULFILLMENT

I am a valued member of my team

> OPPORTUNITIES DON'T HAPPEN, YOU CREATE THEM.

I EASILY FIND SOLUTIONS TO CHALLENGES

> THE ONLY WAY TO DO GREAT WORK IS TO LOVE WHAT YOU DO.

I attract new opportunities effortlessly

"Focus on being productive instead of busy."

I attract new opportunities effortlessly

THE FUTURE DEPENDS ON WHAT YOU DO TODAY.

I maintain a healthy work-life balance

I AM A LEADER IN MY FIELD

3.6. Knowledge: Development and Learning

Write down 10 wishes below related to acquiring new knowledge and skills through courses, workshops, reading books, watching educational videos, attending seminars and webinars.

Examples:

- I've read 12 books on personal growth and development within a year.
- I've mastered my driving skills this year.
- I've successfully completed a programming course.
- I've achieved B2 level of a foreign language.
- I've undergone a series of leadership development programs, which helped me improve my managerial skills and enhance team performance.
- I've attended an international conference in my field of work.
- I've completed a certification course in project management.
- I regularly watch educational videos on graphic design, which significantly improved the quality of my work.
- I've attended a workshop on public speaking, which greatly improved my ability to persuasively present ideas and projects to an audience.
- I've subscribed to and regularly watch an educational channel on investments and financial planning, which helps me better manage my finances.

Knowledge Wish List

○ 1
_____
_____

○ 2
_____
_____

○ 3
_____
_____

○ 4
_____
_____

○ 5
_____
_____

○ 6
_____
_____

○ 7
_____
_____

○ 8
_____
_____

○ 9
_____
_____

○ 10
_____
_____

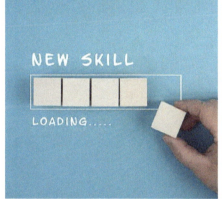

Learn
EMPOWER
Skill
Potential
Winsdom

UNLOCK YOUR POTENTIAL

I TURN INFORMATION INTO ACTION

Learning enriches my life every day

I am constantly expanding my horizons

"Live as if you were to die tomorrow. Learn as if you were to live forever."

I absorb information quickly and effectively

discover

LEARN
FROM YESTERDAY
LEAVE
FOR TODAY
HOPE
FOR TOMMOROW

I apply my knowledge with wisdom

I AM ALWAYS EVOLVING AND IMPROVING

LEARNING is a CONTINUOUS LIFESTYLE

" KNOWLEDGE IS POWER. "

3.7. Family: Strengthening Bonds with Loved Ones

Write down 10 wishes below related to strengthening family relationships, organizing shared leisure activities, trips, etc.

Examples:

- My family is financially secure and well-off.
- My loved ones are healthy and in a resourceful state.
- Every month I organize family board game nights, which has become our favorite tradition.
- I've started a tradition of weekly family dinners, where we share the week's news, discuss plans, and enjoy each other's company.
- I've organized a week-long family trip across Europe.
- My spouse and I have completed a relationship building course.
- I've created a family photo album, gathering photos from all our trips and significant events.
- I've taught my children camping and organized a family hiking trip to the mountains.
- I've given my parents a holiday trip to the sea.
- We've participated in a charity event as a family.

Family Wish List

◯ 1

◯ 2

◯ 3

◯ 4

◯ 5

◯ 6

◯ 7

◯ 8

◯ 9

◯ 10

FAMILY
HAPPINESS
Support
Harmony
Joy

JOY

MY FAMILY IS MY SOURCE OF STRENGTH

My home is filled with love and laughter

HOME Sweet HOME

"FAMILY IS A LIFE JACKET IN THE STORMY SEA OF LIFE."

3.8. Wealth: The Path to Financial Freedom

Write down 10 wishes below related to financial stability and purchases you want to make.

Examples:

- I've paid off all debts and closed my loans.
- I've learned to identify expenses and eliminate them quickly.
- I've achieved total financial stability by creating an emergency fund for 6 months of living.
- I've renovated my apartment.
- I've made my dream trip to a new country.
- I've bought a new phone.
- I've bought the car of my dreams.
- I've saved enough money to buy my own house in the desired area.
- I've invested in purchasing a piece of land for future house construction.
- I've invested $2000 at a 20% annual rate.

Wealth Wish List

○ 1 _____
_____

○ 2 _____
_____

○ 3 _____
_____

○ 4 _____
_____

○ 5 _____
_____

○ 6 _____
_____

○ 7 _____
_____

○ 8 _____
_____

○ 9 _____
_____

○ 10 _____
_____

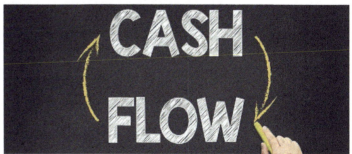

PROSPERITY

ABUNDANCE

FREEDOM

Independence

Wealth

I AM A MONEY MAGNET

MONEY COMES TO ME EASILY, EVEN WHILE I SLEEP

Today I commit to living my financial dreams

> MONEY GROWS ON THE TREE OF PERSISTENCE

I am always discovering new sources of income

FINANCIAL INDEPENDENCE

I am financially free and thriving

I accept and receive unexpected money

I have unlimited abundance

> Working because you want to, not because you have to, is financial freedom.

WEALTH CONSTANTLY FLOWS INTO MY LIFE

3.9. Fame: Recognition and Influence

Write down 10 wishes below related to recognition in your personal and professional lives, public esteem, your qualities admired by others.

Examples:

- I'm the best father/mother/daughter/wife…
- I'm a reliable friend.
- I'm a mentor and friend to my children.
- My children admire my ability to remain optimistic in any situation, which makes me a role model for them.
- My spouse is proud of my attention to detail in everyday life.
- I was recognized as the employee of the year at my company.
- My colleagues admire my ability to see solutions where others see only problems, which made me an innovative leader at our company.
- Clients and partners admire my honesty and reliability in business relationships, making me a respected and trusted partner.
- I inspire others with my passion for education and self-improvement, motivating them to strive for better in their endeavors and seeing me as a role model.
- My students recognize me as the best mentor.

Fame Wish List

◯ 1

◯ 2

◯ 3

◯ 4

◯ 5

◯ 6

◯ 7

◯ 8

◯ 9

◯ 10

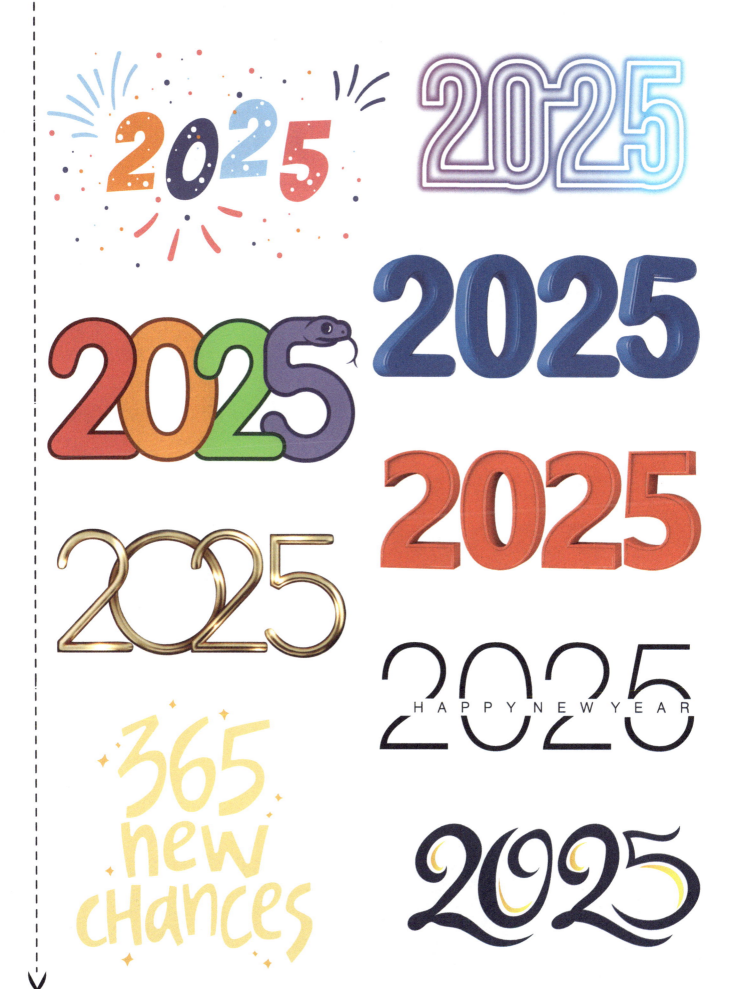

Part 4: Enhancing Effectiveness

4.1. The Practice of Gratitude: The Key to Success

Congratulations! You have successfully created your vision board. Take a moment to appreciate yourself for completing this task. Also, thank the Universe for its assistance. Celebrate your small victory and reward yourself. This celebration will motivate you to move forward and achieve your next goal.

Expressing gratitude for a wish that has already been fulfilled is a powerful way of acknowledging the value of what you already have and recognizing which wishes have been fulfilled. This, in turn, will help enhance your motivation to move forward and achieve new goals.

Here's how you can do Practice of Gratitude:

Create a gratitude ritual. Every time your wish is fulfilled, thank the Universe and those who helped this wish come true. Make the practice of gratitude a regular part of your life.
Ask yourself: **What am I grateful for?**
Take a moment to reflect and appreciate the things you have in your life.

Feel gratitude. Allow yourself to feel genuine gratitude for every wish fulfilled. Think about how these events have impacted your life.
Ask yourself: **How do I feel now that my wish has come true?**
Recognize the positive impact of fulfilling your wishes.

Express your gratitude. If possible, share your gratitude with those who helped you fulfill the wish. This can be a personal message, a thank-you letter, or simply words of gratitude in conversation. You can also do this in your mind or write it down in a gratitude journal.
Ask yourself: **Who am I grateful to and how can I express it?**
Take a moment to appreciate the people in your life who have helped you.

Remember, gratitude is not just about what you receive but also about your attitude to life. Practicing gratitude for fulfilled wishes helps develop a positive and grateful outlook on life, which is a powerful tool for achieving personal happiness and satisfaction.

4.2. The Technique of Powerful Visualization: The Path to Realizing a Dream

The powerful visualization technique is an effective tool that can help us achieve our goals and make our dreams come true. **Use this technique:**

1. Envisage the final result as if it has already happened.
2. Feel joy and gratitude for having achieved what you desired.
3. Consider how your life will change once your wish comes true.
4. Practise daily for 2 to 10 minutes.
5. Be committed to your wish and ready for action.

Why does it work?
Our brain doesn't differentiate between real events and those we imagine. It perceives both scenarios in the same way. For example, just the thought of a lemon already makes your mouth water, because for the brain it's the same whether you are actually eating a lemon or just mentally picturing it.

Remember, when we visualize our desires and sincerely strive for their fulfillment, the Universe inevitably opens up a **"window of opportunity"** for us.

By practicing visualization daily, we tune our brain into finding ways to pursue our desires. This allows us to discover new opportunities and seize them..

The "window of opportunity" includes people, events, financial opportunities, and other resources that help us move step by step towards realizing our dreams.

Conclusion

Finally, I would like to share a mindset that can help you overcome the anxiety and overthinking, **"What if it doesn't work out?"**

We often focus on how we can make money, but sometimes it can come to us in ways we have not yet considered. For example, it could be given to us as a gift. The Universe guides us towards our desires in the shortest and most unexpected ways. We can't envisage the way our dreams come true. Repeat these words to yourself:

It will be my way.
It won't be my way.
It will be better than I expected.

Let these words remind you that even if something does not go as planned, it means that the Universe is guiding us towards a better path. Either way, the outcome will exceed our expectations.

The most important thing is to take action! Just creating a wish list and a vision board is not enough. It is essential to take tangible steps towards achieving them, practise gratitude, and visualize.

Start with the most effortless desires you have written down and let the Universe help you!

Thank You

I'm thrilled to say that we have reached the end of our journey together in creating a vision board to bring your dreams to life. I'm so grateful to you for joining me on this personal and creative path, and I hope that this book has empowered you with valuable insights and practical steps to manifest your visions.

I'd like to take a moment and dedicate this book to my beloved cat, Leo, who has been my friend for 10 years. He was my source of inspiration and support during the growth and transformations that led me to write this, my first book. Sadly, Leo passed away just before the book was finished, but he will always hold a special place in my heart. He taught me how to love unconditionally and I want to share this love with the world.

If you found the techniques and stories in this book helpful, please share your experience! Reviews on Amazon are incredibly important to independent authors like myself. Not only do they help other readers find and benefit from this book, but also provide me with essential feedback to improve and continue creating resources that help you achieve your dreams.

You can leave a review following these simple steps:
1) Visit the product page on Amazon.
2) Scroll to the 'Customer Reviews' section.
3) Click on 'Write a customer review'.
4) Share your thoughts on the book.

Your support means everything to me, and I am immensely grateful for any feedback you provide. Thank you so much for being part of this journey.

Remember, your vision is powerful, and your dreams are worth pursuing.
Keep visualizing, keep creating, and let's make those dreams a reality!

With heartfelt gratitude and best wishes,

Diana Plavnieva

Made in the USA
Las Vegas, NV
25 May 2025